Ameri

Firefighters

by Lena Crawford

HOUGHTON MIFFLIN HARCOURT
School Publishers

PHOTOGRAPHY CREDITS: **Cover** © Bettmann/CORBIS. **1** © Bettmann/CORBIS. **2** © Marilyn Angel Wynn/Nativestock Pictures/CORBIS. **3** Visions of America, LLC/Alamy. **4** © Bettmann/CORBIS. **5** The Granger Collection, New York. **6** © Bettmann/CORBIS. **7** (l) ©SSPL/The Image Works, (r) Heather DiPiazza/Scott B. Rosen Photography/drr.net. **8** © Greg Kieca/Shutterstock. **9** © Leverett Bradley/CORBIS. **10** Karen Moskowitz/Getty Images. **11** © Creasource/CORBIS. **12** © Ariel Skelley/CORBIS. **13** © Richard Cummins/CORBIS. **14** © ChameleonsEye/Shutterstock

Printed in China

ISBN-13: 978-0-547-02422-6
ISBN-10: 0-547-02422-3

14 15 16 17 0940 19 18 17 16
4500569761

Life in America Long Ago

In the 1700s, America was very different. There were no paved streets or tall buildings. Most people were farmers, and they rode horses to get from place to place.

People did not have many of the inventions we have today. For example, there were no gas stoves. There weren't any electric lamps either. People used fire instead. They cooked meals in fireplaces and burned candles so they could see at night.

But if fires got out of control, they caused big problems. Most homes were made of wood, so they burned very easily. Most homes were also close together, so fires could move quickly from one house to another. People needed to do something to protect themselves and their homes.

Fighting Fires Then

The city of Boston was the first to take action. People there bought a fire engine designed in England. They pushed or pulled the engine to a fire. They used buckets to fill a tub with water. Then they pumped the engine to push the water from the tub into a hose. Finally, water sprayed out of the hose. It was a lot of work!

Benjamin Franklin

People in Boston also picked some men to work as firefighters. Benjamin Franklin decided to do something even better in the city of Philadelphia.

Franklin formed a fire brigade, or team, with 30 men. They practiced putting out fires and talked about fire safety. As a result, they were well prepared to fight fires.

When fires broke out, people rang bells and shouted for help. The brigade had its own engine that could be pulled to fires. They used horses to pull the engine to the fire as fast as possible. The firefighters also carried buckets that they filled with water from nearby wells. Then they threw the water at the fire.

Leather bucket

Benjamin Franklin's brigade was called the Union Fire Company. It was the country's first fire department. It was also one of Franklin's greatest accomplishments.

The Union Fire Company achieved a lot of success. Philadelphia became much safer, so other cities soon followed its example.

Fighting Fires Now

Firefighting has changed a lot since those early days. Now firefighters use all kinds of equipment. They ride in trucks instead of on horses. They get water from hydrants instead of wells.

Fire trucks have powerful hoses that can spray large amounts of water. They also have long ladders that reach 100 feet off the ground. Firefighters climb them to reach flames high up in tall buildings.

Today, most firefighters work from fire stations. They keep equipment and trucks inside each station. They also eat and sleep there when they work for a long time.

When a fire breaks out, people call 911 to get help. An alarm goes off at the closest fire station. Firefighters rush to put on uniforms. Then they slide down poles to their truck. They hop aboard and race to the fire.

Firefighting has changed in other ways. Long ago, only men fought fires. Today, women put out fires, too. Some firefighters also help people who are hurt or sick.

Firefighters have always been remarkable heroes. People have written articles and stories about how brave firefighters are. They have even composed songs and made statues in honor of firefighters!

How do you think firefighting will change in the future? What kinds of uniforms will firefighters wear? Maybe fire trucks will fly one day. That will help firefighters save even more lives!

Responding

TARGET SKILL Compare and Contrast

How does firefighting long ago compare to firefighting now? Copy and complete this diagram.

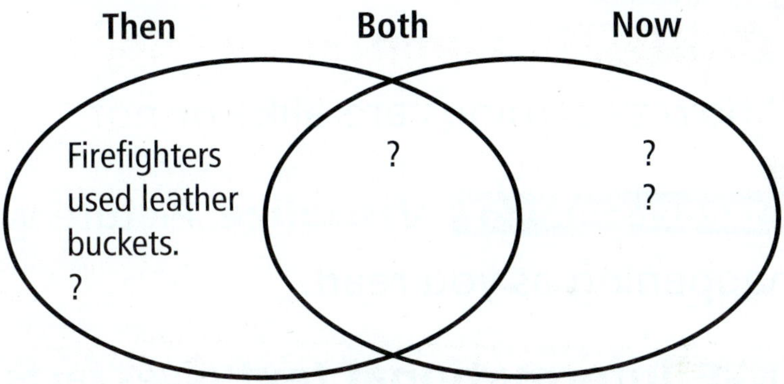

Write About It

Text to World Do you think firefighters should ride on horses or in trucks? Write a paragraph that explains your opinion. Be sure to use opinion words and phrases, such as *should, I think, I feel*, and so on.

TARGET VOCABULARY

accomplishments	**designed**
achieve	**inventions**
amounts	**remarkable**
composed	**result**

TARGET SKILL **Compare and Contrast**
Tell how two things are alike or not.

TARGET STRATEGY **Visualize** Picture what is happening as you read.

GENRE **Informational text** gives facts about a topic.